Love Adrift in the City of Stars

Also by Toni Thomas:

Chosen
    Brick Road Poetry Press

Fast as Lightening
    Gribble Press

Walking on Water
    Finishing Line Press

Blue Halo
    Annalese Press

Ace Raider of the Unfathomable Universe
    Annalese Press

You'll be Fast as Lightning Coveting my Painted Tail
    Annalese Press

Hotsy Totsy Ballroom
    Annalese Press

Love Adrift in the City of Stars

Poems

First published in 2019 by Annalese Press
134 Towngate
Netherthong
Holmfirth
West Yorkshire HD9 3XZ
England

Copyright © 2019 Toni Thomas

Please Note
All characters and situations appearing
in these pages are in the service of poetry.
Any resemblance to real persons,
living or dead, is purely coincidental.

All rights reserved. No part of this publication may be reproduced, stored, or transmitted in any form, or by any means electronic, mechanical or photocopying, recording or otherwise, without the express written permission of the publisher.

Cover by Peter Wadsworth

British Library Cataloguing-in-Publication Data
A catalogue record for this book is available on request from the British Library.

ISBN 978-0-9956652-7-9

Acknowledgements

So many gifted poets have leant their generosity to my development, and for this I remain forever grateful. Very special thanks go to Galway Kinnell, Ilya Kaminsky, Sharon Olds, Brigit Pegeen Kelly, who have inspired and mentored me in invaluable ways. Thank you Nikky Finney for your encouragement, and William Stafford so long ago for believing in me.

Contents

Part One: *Blinded Pixies*

In the forward section	3
I am practicing my Horatio voice	4
You preen the forest	5
Your mouth is an empty ashtray	6
We were not an army of ants	7
You are sharp shooting with destiny	8
I talced our coupledom	9
You blow kisses	10
We are caramelizing the apples	11
Is it easy now to see past fences	12
In the carbon emission test	13
We can give someone a bribe	15
I drape a cloth around love	16
Will the city streets always find us	17
We never wanted to curse fate	18

Part Two: *In the Ringworm grows a Rose*

We have the memory of hard times	21
Are we beauty blind	22
The child next door	23
My brother and I practice our yodels	24
We parade around with our colored cotton	25
My mother never married	26
We ponder hope	27
We are calling back the dead	28
The cremation of the dead	30
There was no shrimp boat	31
In Connemara the stinging nettles	32
Under this awning	33
Sometimes to disarm the past	34
How many people	35
How many mullioned hopes	36

All day I finger the territory	37
The snow queen card	39
The Basilica of Maria de Santo Delgato	40
Someone mutters *it is too late*	41

PART THREE: *Unqualified Lovemaking*

The Brazilian tan that anoints her body	45
I had not yet become vampire girl	46
I stumble from foot to foot	47
I am peeling the past clean	49
All day I've been playing canticles	50
Tomorrow maybe I'll cross the bridge	51
Some men curse fate	52
The birds have fled	53
I called today	54
I have grown happiness	55
I have never liked farewells	56
Does the sun always arrive	57
Do we disavow	58
Busted Victrolas won't always	59
We were coming across the word decency	60
I wanted to proposition	61
There is a confluence to the river	62
There are cruise alleys	63

For Peter
My lucky palomino in the field

On foot
I had to cross the solar system
before I found the first thread of my
red dress.
I sense myself already.
Somewhere in space hangs my heart,
shaking in the void, from it streams
sparks
into other intemperate hearts.

Edith Södergran

Part One

Blinded Pixies

In the forward section

to the history of my life
I pick onion
out of a far field
note-take the cloud cover

the shoe on my left foot
empties of sand
neighbors chortle about blue locust

my father scrapes clean
his angry eye
my mouth chews death down
spits it out
learns it is not so dangerous.

In the forward section
to the history of my life
I arrive some sparkling
resemblance of my once self
as if birds perch in my head
pistols of onion are the impossible
harbingers of spring
get sliced
folded into my poorboy sandwiches
translucent with light.

I am practicing my Horatio voice

the one that colonizes winter
can hypnotize a rabbit
grow sunflowers double girth
bend a fence
beg night angels to instigate a garage band.

I remember how you scoffed
labeled me *piece of duff* in a pint sized world
blinded pixie
as if my eyesight fails
clover no longer suppers with starlight
the birds' mouths sit empty.

I am practicing my Horatio voice
spleen of the past creamed into poplar
my lucky palomino in the field
the broadband rope of the night
spilt open into abigails.

You preen the forest

from a lookout tower on the top ridge
decide what to spare, what to bleed
this sitka stays, the alder goes
keep a broad stick in your hand
steer with direction.

I watch how you sort
get others to oblige
go where you want, do what you say
transfer this skill to marriages
to ours
where to live, what stays, what goes
who gets to keep secrets
who gets voted *crazy*
who wins, who loses
how to get what you need
without expending.

You preen the forest
look for new tracts
untried adventure
invisible the detritus
till there are no blots.

Your mouth is an empty ashtray

doesn't let soot enter
keeps me at arm's length
no messy.

It gets tiresome
being this clean
the blue aerosol
spit polish
lock up of delicate panties.

You lick words
sport apostolic
devour science
suck the uncertain out of forest.

The days of axed dalmatians arrive
professorial wrinkles, grey stubble
when you podium no permanence
become the arbiter of fate
suck the life out of our marriage.

We were not an army of ants

heading in for the kill
paste kingdom before the defeats
were not factory owned
preternatural

didn't fasten our waists around want
pop pills
sound the same words —
embodiment   reinvent   authentic
till they habituate into a slush pile

did not always dot our *i's*
mind our delivery system

but still summer swings into winter
the cat chucks out hair balls
weather attests to the fragility of a roof

still love disavows its slow dance
my negligees grow rust
you make me into a pillbox
turn your voice slippery

as if someone has swallowed a theory
we are no more than want ads
expendable.

You are sharp shooting with destiny

down a bird here, axe handle there.
It is remarkable how obstinate things can be
to let their blood stain
end up a cesspool.

The street grows watchful
houses brace
dogs skittle
children slide into camouflage
sabotage their toast.

I practice new glyphs
a language for after this one
in case we become remaindered
loose adjectives
the hipster city gone snowflake
planet on the run
in a thin space.

I talced our coupledom

till it was powdered bright
smelt of jasmine
no crows.

Is it easy to perpetuate summer
summon a windless grin
palpitate longing till it does a handstand?

No one knew you could break a nose
deal in lies, wax cruel, stay impervious
that under the grin, the charm, the erudite
is a back story of ambushed fields
kegs of wine, late night porn
a briefcase of Viagra.

Sometimes a house gets talced so thick
the rooms crucify
children turn to stone
dogs rust
we beg for attention
mumble something about vows, family
will be reminded of our needy
told to ignore the brunette emails.

Sometimes what we imagine
and what we get are not the same
sit down conversations, begging
are of no use
betrayal rules.

You blow kisses

they are wrapped in plastic bubbles
anchorless
prophesize future, intricate theories
a spotless past
fact filled lovemaking.

I want to believe words are more
than needle and genuflect
can be a thornless plantation
move past proselytizing.

All night the scepters of hope visit me.
Nobody suspects you'll be bit by an asp
end up in hospital
your sharpshooter mind intact
ego bruised
but not exposed.

We are caramelizing the apples

sickly sweet, syrupy
but then some days call for this
thick as billboards that boast
good cognac, blonde vixens
hot sex at the coast
18 carat infinity rings, craft beer.

We had tried ordinary happiness
that overwrought soliloquy
pabulum that passes for designer shoes
monologues the geese
elbows hipster paradise into
a perfect parakeet named Molly.

It is nearly summer.
Time for play drones and ferris wheels
tall grass and short shorts
potted geranium
stretch a dollar into a windfall.

I wonder – can caramelizing apples
be good for the soul
are my lips more than formaldehyde
the entry gate for wet kisses
can they fuel a mouth organ
drink down the sky
turn dessert into more than
a diet language for love
way station beyond betrayal?

Is it easy now to see past fences

dime a dozen our needs
till they rise up on tiptoe
do a curtsy
ask for sweet potato, oysters
tropical cocktail?

I have seen forsythias get up
perform a sway jig before
the rain takes them
hippopotamus schooled
to rise on one heavy foot
crowd please.

Is it easy with practiced elocution
to neon our name
more than a dust storm
pump our body muscular
palomino the sunset

manufacture our slinky
rise up inflammable?

In the carbon emission test

my mother will lose
be pronounced *delinquent*
a vehicle that leaks
plays hooky
is a crash queen.
Others envy her thick copper pageboy
low cut dress, sway of hips
tribe of bracelets.

Every now and then we set off
manned with her blue thermos
cucumber and dill sandwiches
set off with the top down
ribboned thrust
her penchant for a heavy horn
tailgating.

She puts her foot down
the wind is lonely
the black tar needs a workout.

In the carbon emission test
she and I are losers
will not pass
be stamped with the sticker
good for two years
will push midnight into our headlamp
squeeze
cruise out of town
as if nothing deters
no winter
preying wolves
follow us
no hick place without a gas station
rest room, bags of pretzel.
She keeps the hood down
as if rain never paws

the night needs us
looks for a picnic spot
tired intersection
tells me again about the guy last June
who vied to be her summer lover
talks about the late hours the dark keeps

how a 24 hour café in the middle of nowhere
can hold a good grill, bite size view of the hills
carry the world in its fist
serve up Polish sausage, French rolls, seasoned potato
sunset on a supper plate

how the cook will be lean, shaggy, attentive
sexy in his tapered black pants under the white apron
bring out the bottomless coffee
that gives and gives.

We can give someone a bribe

construct a lifeless face, pert lover
double size house, job with premature exits
perfume our rooms, our words, our lives
call them – *self-made* and *prosperity*

still the terrible days of havoc set in
the axe handles and lice
preternatural windstorms
still we long for redemption
something more than the temporal house
blog space, headline, email.

We can give someone a bribe
you oil my hand, I anoint yours
contract a business ceremony of equals

cast a prenuptial balance sheet
till the personal portfolio grows hefty
our presentation is beauty on stilts
words align

till every morning we are a product of
close shave, aerosol
genie in a bottle
the privilege of disregard and pick.

I drape a cloth around love

In June the northwest weather
has its own way
can melt like a sex siren
douse you in hail
puddle the yard
strangle the swing with ivy
and not care.

Does love ever grow cramped
will it still water the plants
stroke the onion field
keep the radio from hissing
bronze into a quantum leap of kisses?

When the newspapers wax sickly
pedestrians flood the mall
when the lawn moans muck raked
children slump
when my husband is off in his elsewheres
minding the women down the road

will you gift me with blue ices
on a stymied day
the colossal homily

be the lover
who never walks away
self satisfied
in a field of brunettes
insures every treason is vindicated
the rain just takes and takes and takes?

Will the city streets always find us

the miracle worker
colony of sequestered roses
billboard that hoists silken bodies
into wine country
commentary of cruise ships

will a marriage of colored lights
the aerial lift of children
Pentecostal daybreak
a past peopled with Aprils
always save
the hours of our discontent be
slammed by a squash racket

will a neat framed version of paradise
the baptismal font
white bread shaved into host
ammunition of pain killers
razzmatazz of a glitter skirt
elevator shoes
our buffed words
the heart that puffs then razors
always save

keep innocent children safe
bee colonies intact
the stars from banishment
the forest from being more than a clear-cut
keep the man with the lit candle
from burning down his own house?

We never wanted to curse fate

give it a once only birthdate
never and never and never
but then the rains came
in hospital parade
muddied the path to the meadow
made it impossible for toy trucks
to climb with traction
for girls in bright wellies
to navigate the stream

the rain that crucifies roses
turns a snow cone into a blood bath.

We stood up and tried to drink
drink down the rain
wash out our voice
so it wouldn't maim
wash out our blue beard fantasies
erase our mothers with their ribboned
summer dresses of hope
backyard clotheslines.

We never wanted to curse fate
just warm it on our fingers
wear it easy as a pocket fan
time fantasy machine
unencumbered midnight

but then the rains came
and you broke my heart.

PART TWO

In the Ringworm Grows a Rose

We have the memory of hard times

iced hands
no snow tires
heating oil near empty
the dogs eating scrap
our potato soup stretched a season
coat hangers and Lenten
promised not to commit suicide
sidestep our life.

I learned basement trunks make a home
when the world forgets us.

We have the memory of hard times.
My mother sang - *In the ringworm grows a rose*
my father drank the neighbor's whiskey
we knit gloves, dreamt a summer playhouse
hauled scrap metal for a buck.

Is it possible to build a world out of nothing
scaffold the past till it shines
a painted egg cup?

I know the space of sideways
how to grow so small
crowbars won't find
arrows don't pierce
words leak no flood plan.

Over time my eyelet has grown ancient
I funeral homicides
succor the old
tell tease children
marry my ear
to the tired echo
of shop floors.

Are we beauty blind

now that the colored flames
look the same
so blonde
bright in their dazzle?
They speak of beach bungalows
sleepless nights at the coast
spaghetti straps
burgundy lips that never razor.

See how the syrah breathes
oysters rise from the shell
travel brochures flap fretless.

Are we beauty sanctified
now that the columbines sing our name
the mirror waxes faithful
our muscular bodies
shimmy into silk
smooth as our legs?

The child next door

devours lemon cake
umbrellas her bent hope inside each slice.
Some lives are made like this – provisional.
They look for handrails
a safe way out, snug shoebox
more than the temporary of crocus
food stamps, a fifth floor walk up
early dismissal.

I have heard of beauty gone for a walk
never come back
and death that gobbles yard swings
stalks showy places, swallows a kiss
lays a brass bell before its come cries
have heard of girls who disappear early
inside cake batter, a sweat shop
in the ecclesiastics of want that is
more than a plate of onion, grilled cheese
as if their lives become invisible
divorced moms, widows
young girls with no clocks.

Can we grow a tunnel
an underground bunker
so thick it saves
are some things preternatural
do they carry the soul
into a forest
beyond
yanked down space?

My brother and I practice our yodels

claims to proficiency
as if they can save
shore up a bridge
keep the stuntman from falling
turn a brothel into the
veranda clad house.

Nobody wants to hear
neighbors shut their windows
the dog turns away
my father blasts Ella.

All day the bugs rise up
snow melts
our mother refuses her deathbed.

My brother and I practice
our yodels, singsong
dig hope out of the locked chest
twine our hair into braids
bake good strudel
help the dark unbutton its sinister.

In the cramped house
disconsolate parlor
her dying room
will our singsong save?

We parade around with our colored cotton

polka dots, seersucker
tied at the shoulder with string
muddied leather sandals
artificially flavored strawberry milk.

It is easy to hold life up and kiss it
when you are five years old
don't care yet what others think
don't understand misfortune
a father's pained voice.

My brother ambitions to ride
the sky with his wheels
defy gravity
later ruts out the yard
jumps higher, faster
ends up an aerial rollercoaster.

We parade around in our colored cotton
run bases, shoot marbles.
I pill my lips around lilac
promise to stay faithful
as if god rainbows the grass
consecrates dirt
never goes missing.

But things happen.
My mother's heart fails
she shatters her blue morning teacup
my brother can't forget her lost voice
dies alone in an anonymous motel room.
My father never learns to sing.
Over time my veil grows spotty
I look for summer in all the wrong places
try to peel you out of a blue orchestra.

My mother never married

the field of ice
blue tinted cocktail
primped version of poodle
never manhandled her hair
to lie flat

somehow kept a faith
life in its fisted abundance
would still travel her
a white arm of beach
green vernacular that spills
kisses heavier then hairnets.

For this she coaxed her body sexy
offers up advice from her deathbed
reminds me of the fair hearted child
who watchdogs the moon
the cottonwood's spindle
how even a dime store ring
can hold its moment of glory
in the damp cup
of our secret lamp shade.

All night I stir amongst the
honey of her voice
its lost tuition
scratch nails.

We ponder hope

turn it around on our pinky finger
talisman of what
not pint size men in the orange grove
the doll that does tricks
purges midnight with her bright curls

not the coin box that feeds the
briny gallop of a metal pony
tarnished soup for the dead
cowlicked hair gone straightly.

We ponder hope
its more than a sweet scent
promise to elope
hint of matrimony
want to feed it mango
tin cups for the deceased

feed it more than
the chromium sunset
someone else packaged
for us.

We are calling back the dead

it is that kind of evening
ouija board
popcorn and lemon cake.

Uncle Amele arrives first
looks older, lots of grey
says he regrets the stroke
misses his three family house in Queens
aunt Bertha's pot roast, grandkids
the one room cabin in the trees
says he has a secret for taming rabbits
won't tell us till we feed him a good meal.

Next comes my mother
still strikingly handsome
the auburn pageboy
body that invites in petal pushers
low dip top.
She no longer needs to cook
paint peel the sunset
warns of rancid milk, hurried children
instructs us to spoon hope into a glass jar
vouchsafe the garden
become blue camouflage
warns the world is addicted
to another kind of sing song.

We are calling up the dead
our hair on end, voices shaky
unsure if what gets said
what we see
is meant to be more than just gray apparition
crush our lives into saintly

unsure what to believe
what to let go
as if our lives are over endowed with voices -

they crowd the radio, billboards
computer screen, television
till it's hard to know what is true
hear my mother speaking
my aunt Bertha's recipe for crumb cake
uncle's secret way with the rabbits

but then, how could I know
they would all die young
be relegated to a Ouija board
blue zone
come to me only when the night
beats its fists
the spirits mentor

that I'd be the only one left?

The cremation of the dead

is done without ceremony
they pull the switch
the oven flames
your brother's bone and flesh
turn into a sack of ashes.

Is it that easy to leave our body
resurrect as a soot bag
velvet pouch

will it take back the bad years
the worn years
the lack of sunsets
the crack cocaine
the treatment programs
the gone for money in America

will it erase the child wild with dreams
who wood ramped our yard
wanted to jump higher, faster
then wings could carry him

will it succor his star struck
girl lonely
forever young at heart
mapless road home?

There was no shrimp boat

travelogue of nets, webbed feet
child's soporific
chronicle of daisies.

We spat and swore
pretended
this *is* midnight
time of pearly swan songs
lounge chairs slumped under the stars
pretended that love rides no hearse
just nights of fish, mango.

There was no shrimp boat
I could latch onto my lines.
You promised forever
that thrifty word that hides diesel
promised mulled wine
many poems.

What did I know of treason
that raider who porn colonies the dark
sets a vampire man on the loose
how some vampires troll
turn the world lame
predator every kiss.

In Connemara the stinging nettles

don't sting
the man with the tapping feet
asks to marry his childhood sweetheart
she agrees
bread rises unperturbed in the brick oven
in the attic apartment a woman sings.

I have lived all my life here
raised on weak elbows, slow speech
raised on wind, slanted rain
slanted sheep.

In winter when scarcity grows a cracked mirror
the bed sheets yellow
when brussel sprouts drag in the mud
none of us dine on thin plates
the cabbage, turnip agree to be stewed
potatoes rise up in the dirt
the boy with the bent arm
gathers rosemary, crushes its aroma
for the sake of the stew.

In Connemara even one fist of potato
can grow a house party
no one will convince me
vampires track our dust
a caved in roof won't mend
whole groves of people
will move, carry only the city as stargaze

no one can convince me
that the man I've met, will marry
doesn't know durable, a loyal gate
will gamble his kisses faithless
turn any bride into a stab wound.

Under this awning

does the shade shelter
shield me from more than the blinding sun
like a ball mitt shields the player's hand
the skin of the orange vouchsafes its juice
the stickpins in my mother's hair hold tight
only to let her long curls spill at dusk
wild as the river

does it shield me indiscriminate
from cattails, well wishes
that firm stable of kisses that once
housed a family dinner table?

Do we fall apart if the light betrays
if whiplash, the over exercised heat wave
pummels
turns us brideless
scorches the hair to cinder
melts the bright face of the
plastic kissing dolls on the sill
turns your man sharp as a knife blade?

Sometimes to disarm the past

is more than to snip the cat's tail
tell the kitchen rodent *there is no food*
curtain a sick room
turn the house back to dirt.

I have watched boys in a hard thirst
snatch the wings off flies
wield them a cruel blow
have seen grown men weep
cowardice turn into a rescue mission
women divorced of their colored thread
crayon a sunset
forests slump under the weight of the bulldozer
gum boots come back to haunt.

The fact is- things matter
chickens get crammed into cages
refugees climb into boats, perish
what we forget, what we become
is more than a small thing, teaspoon of winter.

Sometimes to disarm the past is it possible
to cease the paralytic blow
succor the qualms of fate
with a pear tree?

How many people

patch their lives together
sticker tape as they go
putty the dark so it won't splinter
day-glow loss
deal in cockroaches
too much rent
the provisional
juggle, always juggle
convince themselves mac and cheese is enough.

There are moments our lives want
more than faith
more than antidotal
the threatened tree
extinct species
animals cramped in a cage.

Does a blighted life always come right
turn silver
will the moon shine sure for you, for me
set us up in glow worm bright houses
a spotless lawn, deck chairs
will kindness save

what can I own
what do I owe
what am I asked to share here?

How many mullioned hopes

rest in the folds of tucked away cashmere
in cheap rent rooms
where the shade grows vagrant
matts the sleepwear
till there is no more
dead brother, lost family of kisses?

I have seen crowbars last a lifetime
with no repent
flowers give up their petals
for lack of sun
maidenhair shrivel in the valley
without shade.

How much shade to sanctify a life
stall the blue henchman
pause the girl in her track shoes
vacant the road
cause the rose to rethink
the nature of prosperity
cherish every bloom
unfurl petal by petal
as if the day needs us
this moment is enough?

All day I finger the territory

of my minor keys
forgotten meadow
remember the trek I took past Leadville
over the new snow to an abandoned cabin
where my lover poured steaming cocoa
we ate cheese and chutney sandwiches
kissed, groped, listened to the silence.

All day the claims of the world
the voice that prostitutes April
seemed far away.

Are we here for more than summer tarts
the daily grind of supper plates
well-mannered words
a sex sirened sojourn into midnight
amniotic fluid and crushed ice
more than piglet fantasies
the man who stirs mace into the tap water

are we the conveyer of emails
the punch card employee
intricate systems of retrieve and send
the author of blogs
monkey see as monkey does
sepia mug shot and sangrias
the spray on tan, botox
and *see how amazing my life is*
and *never let me go*
the pressed suit
shiny carved nightingale

are we more than plastic toys
a scheduled cabana of play dates
more than cancer
more than on parole relationships
the stock market

life in the fast lane
as if speed saves
more than the travesty of caged birds
wonder woman able to flap
through space with her steel cape?

All day I soothe the minefields of my life
their faulty tuitions
blue shrapnel
hemisphere of cancers
mind the bright as a button
girl child in the field.
She twines dandelion into a headdress
mothers the flowers
doesn't yet see trampled what she gifts.

The snow queen card

turned up
not that I am well suited
faux fur, patent boots
fragile voice, weepy.

It takes rehearsal time
to shore up the past
be a troubadour
ride your braided pony

rise up
amid roast potatoes, rhubarb
tarnished steeples

anchor love
soft speak

consecrate
a season of swallows
your blue halo.

The Basilica of Maria de Santo Delgato

was built 300 years ago
built by master craftsmen
when time blazed no sword edge
was meant to tribute the Mary queen
remind us of her sanctity
supine words, genuflection.

My cousins grew up in the shadow
of the basilica
pray nightly
every Sunday have white host
slipped on their tongue
are kind, trained to turn
the other cheek.

Some days are holy days
some days are days of lost keys
a molten highway
scant supper
some days sew a song on our sleeve
others a lifetime of sorrow.

The Basilica rests miles from here
in the shadow of eucalyptus
gathers the splintered light
hands of the old women
who keep the altar dustless
refill vases
is an armrest of shade
in a sea of heat.

Someone mutters *it is too late*

as if the clock has struck
a downward beat
the river emptied.

I rise up on tip toe
beyond the past
its quaker oats and killer bees
dying mother in the three-family house

rise up to see past yard toys
plastic painted fence
concrete and handball
the enclosures, foreclosures
disguised bush burning
the have-nots who wait to
flame on a less ambulatory day
palpitate the house.

Someone mutters *it is too late*
as if clocks are apostolic
hold the crème of God on their lips
but it is never too late
never just Shrove Tuesday.

The day has busted open
sunlight then rain
wet margins among the forsythia.
The paper heralds news -
refugee camps, child prostitution
the celebrity singer gunned to death
by a stranger in Orlando
loss and rifles.
So much pain flooding our gates
in the half light of the morning's free fall

it's hard to know what fits
needs to be given away.

I wished the wishing well dry
in the hills outside Arundel.
But that was years ago when we rode
our bicycles over loose country

and I believed the story of the otter
reputed to live in the well
at the Bronze Horse Pub
believed in poets' landscapes
no mercenary view of the coast.

But now we gobble
find it hard to dine on half measure
want the panda to grow a litter
circumvent her cage
for the celebrity movie star to rise up
ageless and capable
forever frisky.

Someone mutters *it is too late*
but it is never too late
never just Shrove Tuesday
in the heart's fruit factory.

PART THREE

Unqualified Lovemaking

The Brazilian tan that anoints her body

may not save
nor the muscled beach legs
silver car with the willing landscape
words that know how to wax bright
interchangeable as a suitcase.

How many layers to a life
foreign countries, forgotten shoes
how many early summers
Aprils when the tulips sat lonely
rehearsal rooms that at first glance
are a brilliant tea service
later turn empty?

The Brazilian tan may not save
nor the chemically treated roof
escape bungalow at the coast
10,000 names salvation slogan
hawked as a blue pendant.

So what will save
more than a dice roll, thin veneer
the porch swing studded with shade
the acropolis of want
razored down to a street mall?

What vouchsafes the heart of the child
keeps a woman's hands from empty
impels the farmer to seed his field
insures the old couple's bed will be
no massacre of springtime

what croissants the soul
impels the chicken to lay eggs
the forgotten boy to rise up
the stone bench to stay firm
willing to carry us?

I had not yet become vampire girl

my teeth still in one place
white, pearly, no anxious fence line.
They spoke of sirened April
bikinied volleyball, tulip fields
flush with lovemaking.

Men came. Tall ones and thin ones
smart ones and the unwise
wanted more than pentecostal
more than candlelight and chaste
wanted the salacious
my button down church service cocktails
no ice.

I had not yet become vampire girl.
That would take years
the memory of stone infested snowballs
broken down apartments
hackneyed sunset
of men who could break a nose
steel the moon
blue voice till the windows shatter.

But now I am dangerous
a gamble
take your chances
pussy cat in ermine
fleet footed nightingale
blood red river
when the night upends.

I stumble from foot to foot

yard to yard
have a habit of stumbling
as if stellar eyesight won't save
or pastel fantasies
that lounge at the coast
the over practiced pronunciation of posies
grey blazers and safe plaid.

I stumble from foot to foot
dream lemon ice
scalloped roadways
melted cheese over broccoli
dream pond frogs, pear cake

dream French kisses
not the dime a dozen variety
stodgy ones that land thick
as squished mud
hold no convertible
no, it's the wear the roof down
jack up the stereo variety
that offer up black leather, a seat for two
freeze your legs but promise *no pilfer*

won't settle for a bean casserole, butter candy
80's hit record
won't hit the *expel* switch so you get hoisted
will explore the mouth's damp geography
caress the girl with the stamping foot
red lips

turn her into a lap dog, blue nymph
till she slides into spike heels
the low cut dress
learns to walk over sewer grates

the ancient bridge
brush storms of blue locust
thigh high in fantasy
without a peep.

I am peeling the past clean

want to call it arroyo
green river
window with a view.

Sometimes we tarnish what we love
turn it into contempt, a tag name
pit bull the dark till it never maims
label a person *disaster* or *needy*
reduce them to the side room
with a busted screen.
I have been reduced to nothing
but a side room, busted screen.

I am peeling the past clean.
Not that crowbarring want saves
a putty smile can torch the mountain
but some things are meant to come
right in this world
like my heart
that is more than a flame thrower
sweater factory
black eyed potato
more than chipped plates
the triangular bride
slipped from her cake perch.

See how the sunset travels my sky
doesn't pilfer
the poplars beside the window glance and wave
birds call my name
how loss can outlive a family
town, nation
pause us in our track
sometimes saves.

All day I've been playing canticles

listen to the lift of beautiful voices
on the stereo
they make me feel better
less territorial
able to high wire the stratosphere
detox pain.

The day feels fledgling
like my life
could expire in a shitload of pieces
or amount to something
staple the moon in place.

Some crystal balls hold us ransom
won't take a sack lunch
pinky finger, half sun
insist we spend and spend
till our whole body is a platter
given over to the thin field.

And does ice really sting
when it slides down my throat
melts over the secret places
will it paralyze words
halt a heart attack
succor my dead mother
beyond oblivion

will you come and lick
as if I am a territory of rivers
steer your orange fish
straight through my thawed estuary?

Tomorrow maybe I'll cross the bridge

to love
pause at her doorstep
arrive with apple, cumquat, pear
a pale version of the past
my body's inkblot of loving senseless

tomorrow I may let my heart breath
open the window

as if sanctity grows on trees
roses stroke the wind for asking
unfold their petaled lips
in the spill of sunset

as if death is bigger than stings
more than your merchant of axe handles

and rain -
just a fleeting keyhole
merciful.

Do some men curse fate

even when it is carrying them
become ambassadors of thirst
abhor glass balls, a gnome kingdom
worship that wears glow wings
sparks the dark into a new language

do they exile what they ignore
cast fate into a wastebasket
as if the invisible ones are nameless
privilege saves
the loud voice
double wide
primped job?

I have seen the well-oiled
perfume their life into prosthetics
a textbook, metal halo

but then, there are cesspools
invisible fissures
the shattered grain field
the ones we forget

the unknown
who rise up more than a deathbed
remember the glory of their cloven hair
mohair wing span
remind us -
life confirms, it abides.

The birds have fled

do they always do this when I arrive
as if the heaviness of my feet disturb
their light float over the porch rail?

But then does heaviness have its gold thrum
weight to lend
like the child who digs up graves
fastens a palm to her sleeve
the wagon that sturdies the milk
my father whose sadness swaddles
the miles of his shoes
or my mother who dropped her weight to the floor
final as a death sack.

Do we ever wake up
no longer weighed down
by the perils of love
its pall mall and thin hosiery
become inured to birds, kisses
the way roses lift their petal lips to the sun
even as the heavy boughs
bend low, burden them?

I have seen backs break
happiness turn into a rusted foot soldier
old people catalog the dark
call back a host of swallows.

They fasten not for bread
but for the singing.

I called today

the thrush unconditional in the yard
my phallic symbol for love
adrift in the city of stars
a straw dog in a sea of contemptuous

but then pie-eyed and poems
must count for something
their feather dusted
clay shoes
the way some girls are a season of no panties
lament married to nosegays.

When they spot cleaned paradise
I wasn't willing
wasn't going to murder soiled sheets
trolls and gimlets
placard a foil celebrity
didn't want to rise up on stilts
as if the dirt never needs me.

Sometimes trees are the best place to hide
inside the dry wood of Japanese maple
behind tall cedar, sitka.

Then what will you say about marrying me
the way storyboards lie
cursed tuitions turn lavender
how our bodies sing
in a wind tunnel
a being can turn pearly
even in shade?

I have grown happiness

unstable plant of my youth
that walks undeterred
battle wounded
is sometimes world weary
sometimes a shiny sword
slump pumps the day to marry me
turns axe handles into kisses
blue eyelet

won't settle for no
a death wish
callous the old man's fruitful
armor the park pigeons
won't dim the girl's fantasy
of a new dance hall

is never a dismal failure
too motley

memorizes lemon ice
shorebirds
Amelia's recipe for bread pudding.

In this kingdom of the heart in my palm
life is more than a credit card history
cheese factory
scented monologue.

I have never liked farewells

nasty words, death sentences
they speak of a strapless version of lovemaking
one horse towns, clandestine hope
see you some other year in St. Louis.

What did I know about exits
the toy sheep dug into a dirt burial
lost handmaid
how the sun's face gets swiped
turns into a family of arm wrestles

what did I know about pabulum words
wire coat hangers
burnt sheets, lost asphodel
the way some men fasten conquest
to their wings like privilege.

Let the wind bleed then.
November set up its screw turns.
I will carry an ocean.
Find summer in a snow field.

Does the sun always arrive

a little late
after our hope shrivels
after the voice grows bog deep
takes on its coarse matt
scrap coat
children forget us

after the armloads of defeat
apostrophes
amplitude gone rusted

how many years to uncloak a life
practice April
as if the tire factories of the world
wait on our heart's clearest nectar
unqualified lovemaking?

Do we disavow

the territories of loss
that grieve us
wait on better days
when our eyesight clears
the couch is spacious
we are more than
disguised shipwreck
secret weeping?

I have seen pie in the sky
turn into a simple supper table
a collar of faux fur become
the soup kitchen that feeds.

Do the lost and lonely
learn how to somersault
over blue asphalt
hold a maud moon in their teeth
speak in a quiet language
different
from this one?

Busted Victrolas won't always

play an adagio
hold the world spellbound
but in the postage size house
with enough sticky tape, spit polish
it is possible to crank a tune out of
forgotten woodwork
turn a threadbare armrest into Coltrane.

Late night my mother is up on her stepladder
painting the parlor walls black
when musicians appear out of nowhere
travel through our screen door as if
we are special, the Starlight Lounge
Blue Bunny Club
satisfy my mother's want to turn
her hips into samba.

We peek through a crack
watch them set up their keyboard, sax, drum kit
watch my father offer his dime store version of cocktail
taco chips, salsa
my mother shimmy into her low cut dress
explode in the cramped space
as if the New York ballroom where they first met
is not miles away
and tonight she is vetted in shapely satin
cooed, ogled
will never succumb to heart failure.

Tonight she is deathless
hips shimmying
sublime.

We were coming across the word decency

the one people sometimes shove
in a pat wool suit, buffed shoes
behind a bright picket fence
no variegated woodpecker
uncommon word
pinned loose onto midnight.
Sometimes it lays in small crevices
observes the wind
drinks soporific from a pink straw.

It has been a long time since
your cruel voice was coining
that matter of fact dismissal of dreams
its brunette merrymaker and shape shift
reminding me of my indigent.

Some words are antidotal
some wear comfrey, a warm clothe
turn worship into more than a side note.
Some will flood a house
taunt a heart into ruin
abscond with the furniture
the children.

We were coming across that word decency.
And I have known rye fields in winter
a surfeit of corn
have known seasons with a house gutted
stick bats and napalm

kisses that defy loss
come back thick as a hedgerow.

I wanted to proposition

heart of my heart
stay close
but then the floods set in
and the preternatural past
with its hangnails, collateral poems
lopsided boat
and my mother sunk in her pale dress.

I wanted to halt the tide
till you stepped ashore
bountiful
armed with your ukulele
fresh fruit from the Azores.

There are kisses we mind
with a careful mien
and kisses that are spilt open cargo
an unruly path to the river.
The second ones are the kind I like best -
unbridled peonies
never housebound
pinned to the abject refusal
to ride on a hearse's nameplate.

I want to proposition –
heart of my heart
stay close
as if you are cashmere
my gull with the prize fish

as if anything and everything
is about to arrive for us.

There is a confluence to the river

it never just spends
commits adultery.

My life will always be more
than its tattered seams
more than call worship
the bite sized room
incubators of want
blue neon.

Sometimes I fumigate
reorder the slogans
plaster bright a ball park
reorder my shoes
their catalog of rutted edges
that strut bold imp
uneven bride.

Sometimes ecclesiastics
won't save
I mind no store
no past
no desultory born of plastic roses.

There is a confluence to the river.
In the heliotrope of my widest vision
only your green verdant landscape
in my soul
stays.

There are cruise alleys

and slow lanes
toothpicked homilies
lovers so cumbersome
their words kill
cankered roads
and yes - my dress
its layers of vice
taffeta, broken thread.

Have I kept my best surprises for last
put them in a poor box
with caster oil, honey
kept my hair pinned over
your gated threshold?

But now my body spins
splays petals across blue sky.
Even the starlings want to marry me.

Darling – to reduce me so small
was more than the mote in your eye
a death sentence
was an ignorance of the knowledge
of free falls
of girls who fly out of the flannel city
into space
unsullied as night angels.

Toni Thomas lives in Portland, Oregon. Her poems have been published in Austria, Spain, New Zealand, Canada, England, Scotland, and Australia. In the United States her work has appeared in over fifty literary magazines including *Prairie Schooner, North Dakota Quarterly, Hayden's Ferry Review, the Minnesota Review, Notre Dame Review, Poetry East*, and more. She has published seven collections of poetry and two children's books.

Her figurative clay sculptures have been shown in gallery exhibits in Portland and Chicago, displayed in literary magazines, and housed in private collections in the U.S. and England.

Her short documentary *One of Us* was shown at the Trans-ideology: Nostalgia festival in Berlin and at the Museum of Contemporary Art in Taipei.

Since Toni loves to create and sits buried in reams of poems, manuscripts, clay figures and images....she likes to imagine all of them out in the world, swaying wild as the lupine.

tonithomaspoetry.com

www.ingramcontent.com/pod-product-compliance
Lightning Source LLC
Chambersburg PA
CBHW030457010526
44118CB00011B/980